The
Rain Forests
of the Pacific
Northwest

Ecosystems of North America

The Rain Forests of the Pacific Northwest

Deborah A. Behler

BENCHMARK BOOKS

MARSHALL CAVENDISH
NEW YORK

With thanks to Dr. Dan Wharton, Central Park Wildlife Center, for his careful reading of the manuscript.

Benchmark Books
Marshall Cavendish Corporation
99 White Plains Road
Tarrytown, New York 10591-9001

Library of Congress Cataloging-in-Publication Data
Behler, Deborah A.
     The rain forests of the Pacific Northwest / Deborah A. Behler
          p. cm. — (Ecosystems of North America)
     Included bibliographical references (p.).
     Summary: Provides an overview of the rain forests of the world and describes the rain forests of the
Pacific Northwest and the life that they support.
     ISBN 0-7614-0926-2
     1. Rain forest ecology—Northwest, Pacific—Juvenile literature. [1. Rain forest ecology—Northwest,
Pacific. 2. Ecology—Northwest, Pacific.] I. Title. II. Series.
     QH104.5.N6 B44   2001   577.34'09795—dc21   99-051653

Photo Credits

Photo research by Candlepants, Inc.
Cover photo: Corbis / Galen Rowell
The photographs in this book are used by permission and through the courtesy of: Corbis: Stuart
Westmorland, 6–7, 32–33, 43; Charles Mauzy, 11, 24–25, 40–41; Pam Gardner, Frank Lane Picture Agency,
14; Pat O'Hara, 16–17, 52–53 back cover; Jim Zuckerman, 18; David Muench, 20; Kevin Schafer, 22;
Wolfgang Kaehler, 27; Chase Swift, 28; Joel W. Rogers, 29; Joe McDonald, 31; Tom Bean, 34; Larry Lee, 35;
John McAnulty, 37; Kennan Ward, 39; Ric Ergenbright, 50; Gary Braasch, 55; Warren Morgan, 57. Animals
Animals: Donald Specker, 45; David Boyle, 47; Victoria McCormick, 48–49.

Printed in Hong Kong
6   5   4   3   2   1

Contents

North America's Rain Forest

Imagine yourself entering a cool, damp cathedral of tall **conifers**, such as pines and firs. The ground is padded with tiny **lichens**, a plant that combines **fungus** and algae. Delicate **ferns**, plants with leaflike fronds, hug the moist ground. The trees are draped with **mosses**, plants lacking roots. All of this lush vegetation muffles the sounds of water constantly dripping and flowing.

When most people hear the term *rain forest*, they think of the humid tropical jungles of Brazil, crisscrossed with vines, splashed with bright flowers, and inhabited by jaguars, boa constrictors, and howler monkeys. Many people are surprised to find out that there is a rain forest in North America. The plush, velvety-green **temperate** rain forest of the Pacific Northwest, with its mild climate, is an ancient forest. It runs in a thin green line for 1,200 miles (1,931 km) from Washington State through the Canadian province of British Columbia to Glacier Bay in Alaska. The Pacific

Graves Creek Waterfall in Olympic National Park. The streams of the Pacific Northwest rain forests are rich in nutrients, which are the first link in many aquatic food chains.

Ocean lies on the western side of the rain forest, and the Cascade and Coast mountain ranges lie on the east. Although much of the Pacific Northwest rain forest has been cut for its timber in recent years, the surviving patches have stayed virtually unchanged for about 12,000 years, since the last of the ice ages.

What's a Rain Forest?

As their name implies, all the rain forests of the world share a common component—rain, or at least constant moisture. Rain forests are inundated with water, as much as 200 inches (500 cm) in a year. In a tropical rain forest, the moisture tends to fall evenly throughout the year, though there may still be a relatively wet and dry season. Temperate rain forests have two seasons. One long wet period is followed by a fairly dry summer during which fog provides added moisture. What further distinguishes temperate rain forests from tropical ones are temperature and diversity. In a tropical rain forest, the air temperature remains high year-round, ranging from 77 to 95 degrees Fahrenheit (25 to 35° C). Temperatures in the temperate rain forest rarely fall below freezing but also rarely rise above 80 degrees Fahrenheit (27° C).

Tropical rain forests generally consist of **evergreens** that keep their leaves year-round, such as figs and palms. These forests have a great **biodiversity**, or variety, of plant and animal **species**, groups of organisms that closely resemble each other. A temperate rain forest has less variety but supports a tremendous amount of plant life. The mild and wet winters in the Pacific Northwest make it possible for the most common trees—evergreen conifers such as Sitka spruce, western hemlock, western red cedar, and Douglas fir—to grow incredibly tall, becoming among the tallest trees on Earth. These giants can grow taller than 200 feet (60 m), measure 40 feet (12 m) around, and can live for more than five hundred years. It would take about eight people, holding hands, to encircle one of these magnificent trees.

In the temperate rain forest, massive trunks rise dozens of feet toward the sky before the first branches appear. The **canopy**, or top layer of branches, has multiple levels and is punctuated by standing dead trees, called **snags**. Sunlight filters through the canopy to reach

The Rain Forests of the Pacific Northwest

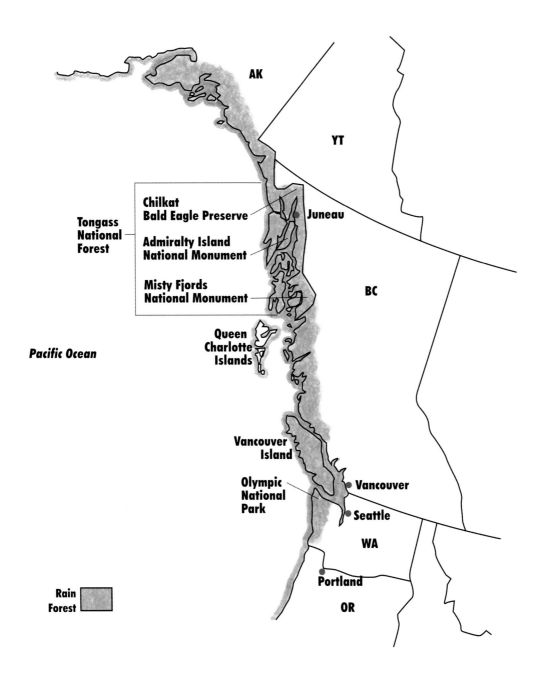

To some, the term rain forest *conjures images of tropical foliage and life near the equator. But another rain forest, North America's temperate one, stretches more than 1,200 miles (1,931 km) from Washington to Alaska.*

the forest floor, which is dotted with large rhododendrons, vine maples, and along streams, big-leaf maples. The ground is littered with leaves and the rubble of fallen, decaying trees that are overgrown with mosses, lichens, ferns, and even sapling conifers. Decomposing logs are vital to the continued regrowth of the forest, as they add **nutrients**, organic molecules, to the soil and create an ideal place for seeds to sprout. These dead trunks with mini gardens growing on them are often called **nurse logs**. A 50-foot (15-m) log may be covered with hundreds or thousands of plants. In some areas, you might see trees of a similar size growing in a row. They all sprouted at the same time on one of these logs.

The rain forest of the Pacific Northwest flourishes because it lies so close to the ocean. The drenching storms that nourish the forest sweep across the ocean eastward from Japan. When the clouds reach the coast, they meet a chain of mountains and rocky islands. Nearly all of the clouds' moisture falls on the western slopes because, as the clouds rise to cross the mountain peaks, the cooler air of the higher elevation causes the water vapor to condense and fall as rain. In summer, warm air in the valleys draws in fog from the coast. So the forest here certainly doesn't suffer from a lack of water.

The sturdy conifers have developed a variety of **adaptations**, or special characteristics, that help them survive the wet winters and dry summers. For example, conifers are evergreen and do not lose their leaves all in one season. This means they can produce food year-round through **photosynthesis**, the process by which green plants make their own food by using the energy of sunlight, carbon dioxide from the air, and water. In another adaptation, the conifers' needlelike leaves have little exposed surface area to allow evaporation. The needles are also densely distributed on the tree, and the tight clumps help retain moisture. Even the shape of the tree contributes to its survival. The cone shapes of the Sitka spruce and Douglas fir allow heavy snow to slide off the branches. If the tree branches grew horizontally, snow would build up and become too heavy, causing the branches to break.

However, the Pacific Northwest rain forest is made up of more than trees. The rain forest is an **ecosystem**, a biological community

Some fallen trees become nurse logs, host to the next generation of plants.

of plants and animals that interact with the nonliving parts of their **environment**, such as the rain and wind. Many species of wildlife thrive in the temperate rain forest, though the animals are not as easy to find as they might be in the Tropics. There are no colorful parrots cawing or monkeys screeching in the trees. The animals of the temperate rain forest are adept at **camouflage**, using color or certain behaviors to hide or blend into their **habitats**, the places where they live. For example, the snowshoe hare has white fur in the winter to match the color of the snow. In the summer, its fur turns brown to make the hare blend in with the leaf litter on the ground. Camouflage is equally important to the hare's **predator**, the great horned owl. The owl's mottled gray and brown coloring makes it hard to see against the tree's bark. If the snowshoe hare could see the owl coming, it would quickly escape—and the owl would go hungry.

Layers of the Forest

A habitat provides the food, water, and shelter that a species needs to survive. In the Pacific Northwest rain forest, different habitats are found at each layer of the ecosystem. Starting at the very top of the forest, the first layer is the upper canopy, or **emergent layer**. There, among other birds and animals, you will find a seabird called the marbled murrelet. The murrelet builds its nest in old-growth forests in the Pacific Northwest. In the early 1970s, ornithologists, scientists who study birds, were amazed when they discovered a murrelet nesting high in a Douglas fir tree. During the day, just like other seabirds, the murrelet flies out to the ocean and feeds on small fish and invertebrates. But at dusk, unlike its close relatives that roost in island burrows, the murrelet returns to its nest on a large branch high in the canopy.

The next layer in the temperate rain forest is comprised of both the middle and lower canopies—home to many species, including the chickaree, or Douglas squirrel. This reddish gray squirrel is active year-round, scurrying through the trees gathering cones, nuts, and seeds. As the cones mature in the fall, the chickaree snips them off at such a rapid rate that it may seem to be raining pinecones. In summer, this squirrel builds a nest of mosses, lichens, and shredded

How Organisms Fit into Niches

The temperate rain forest's varied layers house different habitats in which a wide range of species can establish niches.

The chickaree, or Douglas squirrel, travels through the conifers, collecting cones and hiding them for future use. This behavior helps disperse the trees' seeds to different areas of the forest.

bark that looks like an untidy ball near a tree trunk. In winter, it retreats to holes in the trees.

The **understory**, or shrub layer of the forest, includes plants that produce berries, such as huckleberries and currants. These berries are eaten by mule deer, elk, and smaller animals. After the animals have eaten the berries, the seeds pass through them and are deposited on the ground in their waste matter, sometimes a great distance from where the original plant grew. Thus, animals help to scatter the plants throughout the forest.

The last layer of the rain forest is the moist ground, which provides habitats for reptiles, **amphibians**, slugs, and insects. If you turn over a rock or a piece of rotting bark, you might find a northern alligator lizard. This reptile likes cool, damp places where it can hunt for insects, spiders, millipedes, and snails.

People and the Forest

Native Americans have lived in the Pacific Northwest for centuries, fishing and hunting for food and using the forest for wood and other products. When settlers arrived in the early 1800s, trees blanketed 70,000 square miles (181,000 sq km) of rugged hillsides and valleys. The pioneers thought the forest was endless and began chopping trees to build houses and to clear fields, just as they had done in the East. Later, timber companies and the United States Forest Service **clear-cut** vast areas, removing all the trees to obtain this valuable wood. Today, more than 85 percent of the original forest has been destroyed. The loss of this much of the Pacific Northwest rain forest also spells disaster for many habitats, which may ultimately lead to the extinction of many native wild species.

The temperate rain forest of the Pacific Northwest is extremely important to our own health and the health of our planet. This rain forest, like the tropical rain forests, helps to maintain the planet's biodiversity. It provides habitats for commercially important animals and plants, such as salmon and pines. The rain forest also provides recreational opportunities, such as hiking and bird-watching. In the following chapters, you will explore this intriguing forest, layer by layer. You will learn how it affects you and how people affect it in turn. On your tour of the rain forest, you will visit some parks that you might see in person someday.

In the coastal Pacific Northwest, Native American tribes, such as the Haida, used the western red cedar tree to make more than two hundred types of tools and artifacts. Haida women and children made baskets from the bark and roots. The bark was even used for towels and diapers. The men carved huge totems from the tall, straight trunks.

Life at the Top

For our first stop, let's head for the Olympic National Park in Washington State, one of the most interesting places—and certainly the easiest to get to—along the Pacific Northwest coast. We will look for the species that have established their habitats high in the treetops.

Olympic National Park is located on the Olympic Peninsula in northwestern Washington across Puget Sound from Seattle. The park covers slightly less than 1 million acres (405,000 ha). It could almost be considered three parks rolled into one. The Olympic Mountains rise in the middle of the park, and more than 260 glaciers can be found on the highest peaks. Mount Olympus is the tallest peak at nearly 8,000 feet (2,438 m). In another part of the park, a scenic strip of rain forest runs for nearly 60 miles (100 km) along the Pacific Ocean. Huge rocks and trees litter the beaches that border this section of rain forest.

We are headed for the third and largest part of the park—the temperate rain forest that grows on the western side of the Olympic Mountains. The forest is located in the Hoh, Quinault, and Queets River valleys, not too far from the coast. Trees grow big and tall here. The dominant species that form the emergent

Clouds roll in from the ocean and hit the western slopes of the coastal mountain ranges. As they rise into the cooler air, they drop their moisture in the form of rain, keeping the forest rich in moisture.

On the Olympic Peninsula, huge trunks rise 50 to 100 feet (15 to 30 m) into the air before the first branches appear.

layer are Sitka spruce, western hemlock, red cedar, and Douglas fir.

Sitka spruce grow only in the temperate rainforest ecosystem. They lose considerable moisture from their needles and depend on the fog from the ocean to replenish it. Sitkas grow in a narrow strip along the coast, extending no more than 30 miles (48 km) inland. Douglas fir tolerate slightly drier conditions, and in some parts of the rain forest, they outnumber all the other tree species. One Douglas fir in the Queets Valley measures 298 feet (91 m) tall. That is as tall as a twenty-story building. The first thing you notice when you enter the Pacific Northwest rain forest is how small you are in comparison to the trees. It is somewhat like standing on a street corner in New York City and looking up at the towering buildings. But in the rain forest, there are no honking cars nor rushing pedestrians. It is much quieter. In fact, about all you hear is water dripping off branches and running in streams. More often than not, it is raining in the Pacific Northwest. The temperate rainforest ecosystem receives from 140 to 167 inches (360 to 420 cm)—that is 12 to 14 feet (3.6 to 4.2 m)—of precipitation every year.

Much of the moisture from the fog and rain is trapped in the emergent layer, or canopy, the area above the forest floor where the crowns of the tallest trees meet. In the temperate rain forest, the emergent layer consists of trees that have taken two hundred to three hundred years to develop. Forest canopies are important because they contribute to the health of the entire ecosystem. To start with, much of the forest's photosynthesis takes place here, as the canopy is the first place sunlight strikes. Some of the forest animals, birds, and insects eat the leaves, absorbing the energy. As other leaves fall to the ground and **decompose**, or decay, they add nutrients to the soil to help other plants grow.

The canopy also acts as a buffer between the soil and the atmosphere. If all the rain that falls in this forest were to hit the ground, the soil would **erode**, or wash away. The canopy filters the rain through its network of branches and leaves so that the water falls more gently on the soil. The canopy also shades the forest floor, providing habitats for organisms that need less sun by inhibiting the growth of plants that need large amounts of light.

Hall of Mosses

One of the short trails through the Hoh Rain Forest is appropriately called the Hall of Mosses. Being in the rain forest is indeed like being in a grand hall. Instead of chandeliers hanging from the ceiling, however, we find **epiphytes**, plants that grow on other plants. The

The Hall of Mosses features epiphytes that drape and dangle from seemingly every branch.

epiphytes are supported by the branches of the canopy instead of being rooted in the soil. How do these plants survive so high up? The crown of a single Douglas fir has 60 to 70 million needles. The surfaces of all these needles trap not only moisture from the rain and fog but the nitrogen in dust particles carried by the wind. Epiphytes such as mosses, lichens, and liverworts take advantage of the sunlight, moisture, nitrogen, and other nutrients in the canopy. They grow in

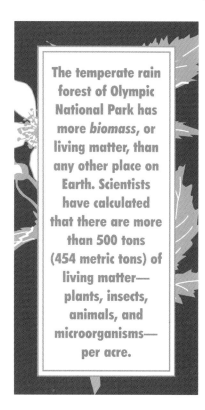

great numbers high above the ground. The enormous branches of a 300-foot-tall (91-m) Sitka spruce can support entire colonies of these "hanging gardens."

More than 130 species of epiphytes live in the Hoh Valley trees. Scientists studying a kind of lichen called lobaria, which looks like leaf lettuce, have estimated that one acre of the rain forest may have 400 pounds (181 kg) of the lichen growing in it. Sometimes pieces of lobaria fall to the ground and are eaten by elk and other browsing mammals. As the epiphytes, lichen, and other plants die, they create thick mats of decaying vegetation that provide places for other plants to take root.

People often wonder if these plants hanging off the branches harm the host trees. The answer is no, except when a branch weakened by disease or damaged by storms accumulates a really heavy load of plants and breaks off. Epiphytes can even be beneficial. Some trees send out special roots to absorb nutrients from the debris that the epiphytic plants leave in the crooks of branches.

The temperate rain forest of Olympic National Park has more *biomass*, or living matter, than any other place on Earth. Scientists have calculated that there are more than 500 tons (454 metric tons) of living matter— plants, insects, animals, and microorganisms— per acre.

Whoooo Lives Here?

The forest canopy also provides specialized habitats for animals. In the temperate rain forest most of the animals can be found on the ground, but some species spend their lives in the canopy, and a few never descend to the ground at all. Probably the most famous animal that makes its habitat in the treetops of the temperate rain forest is the northern spotted owl. In the early 1990s, this species became a symbol of the fight between the logging industry and environmentalists who wanted to save the old-growth forests. Northern spotted owls depend on the canopy of old-growth forests for nesting and breeding. In order to mate successfully and gather enough food for their young, a single pair of owls requires about 100 acres (40 ha). This area must include older trees, such as huge Sitka spruce and Douglas fir, which grow only in the temperate rain forest.

Northern spotted owls spend a great deal of the day sitting quietly in shady trees. You could be standing directly under an owl and never know it was there. They hunt at night, usually for flying squirrels and other small mammals. Their broad, short wings help them maneuver through the maze of branches in the canopy.

The northern spotted owl has been declared an endangered species for two reasons. It is threatened by the logging of old-growth trees that provide its nesting sites, and it is being crowded out by the barred owl. The barred owl is not dependent on old-growth forests and has recently expanded its range in the Pacific Northwest. As a result of these various pressures, fewer than one hundred pairs of northern spotted owls now live in Olympic National Park.

The owl or the tree? The cause of a serious debate, these small birds, northern spotted owls, had staked their claims on the old-growth forest long before the arrival of loggers.

A few species of smaller, perching birds share the northern spotted owl's habitat in the emergent layer of the forest. Most of these birds are insect eaters. The varied thrush, a robinlike bird, perches at the tops of conifers and sings its haunting two-note song. Hammond's flycatcher can be seen looping out from high in the evergreens to catch insects. Townsend's and hermit warblers may also forage and nest in the treetops. The white-winged crossbill feeds high in the canopy on seeds from the cones of Douglas fir and other conifers. As its name implies, the upper and lower parts of its bill are crossed. This adaptation helps it remove seeds from between the scales of cones.

It's not always easy to see the species that live high in the canopy of the temperate rain forest. Scientists often build sturdy platforms where they can watch these interesting animals and plants and learn how they have adapted to life at the top. A blend of birds and epiphytes, the canopy is a sheltered world whose inhabitants have evolved to thrive high above the ground.

Nearly all red tree voles live in Douglas fir trees, sometimes never leaving the tree where they were born. This small mammal builds complex nests of twigs, leaf parts, and other material cemented together with dried feces and urine. Generations of voles may share the same nest site, which functions like a condominium built 150 feet (46 m) up in a tree.

In the Shadows

*T*he Quinault Rain Forest in the Olympic National Park is another excellent example of a temperate rainforest community. It is located in the extreme southern end of the park, near the border between Washington and Oregon. If we take the loop road up the Quinault Valley and around Quinault Lake, we can see an interesting cross section of the middle and lower canopies.

Not only do the plants and animals that live in the temperate rain forest need trees, they need trees at all stages in their life cycles. That means dead trees as well as those covered with needles or leaves. The next layer of the rainforest ecosystem is the middle and lower canopies. Here, the diversity of life is greater than at the tops of the trees. Why? The answer lies in the varied habitats these layers support. Sitka spruces and western hemlocks don't have deep root systems so they can be easily toppled by heavy winds. And their tops can be snapped off by storms. This creates openings in the upper canopy that allow some sunlight to reach the lower levels of the forest. Sunny glades here and there result in trees of uneven heights, different ages, and more diverse species. These varied

In the Quinault Rain Forest, the trees are only as strong as their system of roots.

groupings provide habitats for an array of creatures. Because these canopy levels are not up quite so high, it's easier for us to see animals and plants that make their homes here.

Tiers of Trees

Deciduous trees, which shed their leaves every fall, thrive in this layer of the rain forest. In an opening created where a huge Sitka spruce toppled over, we see the Pacific dogwood. This tree can reach heights of 100 feet (30 m), but that is rare. This pretty dogwood never reaches the tops of the conifers in the emergent layer 200 to 300 feet (61 to 91 km) up. Like the flowering dogwood that grows in the East, it produces bright berries, which birds such as thrushes and band-tailed pigeons depend on for food in the fall. The birds in turn spread the seeds in their waste after the berries have passed through their digestive systems.

The many streams running through the forest are home to the big-leaf maple. As its name implies, this tree has immense leaves, up to 1 foot (30 cm) in diameter. The leaves help collect water dripping from the emergent layer. In the fall, they turn a lovely yellow-orange before they drop off and gather on the forest floor. This species supports even larger amounts of epiphytic plants than conifers do. One of the more common epiphytes that finds a habitat on the big-leaf maple is club moss. Though it looks a lot like moss, this plant is more closely related to the ferns. Huge swags of club moss hang from the maple. And although it appears intrusive, club moss actually benefits the big-leaf maple. If you were to lift up one of these green curtains, you would most likely find whole networks of maple roots that are absorbing nutrients from the mat of moss.

What Good Is a Dead Tree?

You wouldn't think a dead tree would be important to the forest ecosystem. Yet trees that have died and are still standing, called snags, provide critical habitats for a great variety of forest species. Snags decompose from top to bottom and from the inside out. They often become hollow long before they fall to the forest floor. Bats sleep the day away under loose pieces of bark. Birds make nests in hollows.

Locked in a symbiotic, or mutually beneficial, relationship, club moss and big-leaf maples form a partnership that maximizes their chances of survival.

Once seriously threatened, the bald eagle is making a comeback in the Pacific Northwest.

Bald eagles and owls perch atop the snags to eat their prey. The osprey often chooses the top of a very tall dead tree as the site for its massive nest of sticks.

During the summer, dead and live trees at the various canopy levels are abuzz with all kinds of insects. These attract songbirds—warblers, orioles, tanagers, and flycatchers—that breed and raise their young in these northern forests. One bird, Vaux's swift, is commonly seen darting about in a continual search for insects. Swifts are built for speed and agility in the air. Their streamlined bodies are shaped like a cigar, their wings are curved, and they spend so much time in the air that they barely use their tiny feet. Most other swift species nest in chimneys, but the Vaux's swift depends on dead trees in the old-growth forest for its nest sites. This bird spends the winter in tropical forests in South America and then flies all the way to the Pacific Northwest to find snags in which to lay its eggs and raise its young. It prefers trees that are tall and hollow, at least 2 feet (60 cm) in diameter. That gives the bird plenty of room to build its nest and attach it to the inside of the tree with saliva. Unfortunately, the Vaux's swift is in danger of becoming extinct because both its winter and summer forest habitats are disappearing.

One of the prettiest birds in the midcanopy is the chestnut-backed chickadee. This noisy bird often travels in flocks, moving quickly through an area searching branches, bark, and cones for tiny insects. Its call sounds like "buzzy dee-dee." Chestnut-backed chickadees nest in snags as well as in small cavities they hollow out of the trees.

Among the largest birds that we will find living in this layer of the forest is the pileated woodpecker. You will probably hear this bird long before you see it. It makes loud drumming sounds as it drills its large beak into snags and dead branches, looking for beetle grubs and ants hidden in the rotting wood. The best time to look for the pileated

Most pileated woodpeckers spend their entire lives in trees, circling the trunks in search of insects. Their long beaks are effective at boring deep into the wood.

woodpecker is early in the morning. Though this woodpecker measures about 15 inches (38 cm) in length and has a bright red crest, it can be surprisingly secretive and difficult to spot. If the woodpecker sees you, it will quickly move to the opposite side of the tree. Pileated woodpeckers are important because they excavate holes in rotting timber. These holes are used as nesting sites by small rodents and by other birds, including small owls, swallows, bluebirds, and wrens.

One of those rodents may be a northern flying squirrel. Flying squirrels do not really fly. They glide on flaps of skin that stretch from their front legs to their hind legs. The skin functions much like a parachute. Flying squirrels are nocturnal, or active at night. As they glide among the trees, their huge eyes help them find insects, seeds, and lichens to eat.

Aerial Pursuits

During our visit to the rain forest, we will be extremely lucky to see the marten, a large weasel that has a doglike face, a long thick tail, and cinnamon-colored fur. It sometimes feeds along streams but spends most of its time in the varied levels of the canopy. Quick and agile, this mammal preys on red squirrels and can travel for miles through the trees without descending to the ground. A pair of martens may have a home territory that covers 15 square miles (39 sq km).

You also have to look really hard to find the nest of the rufous hummingbird. This tiny bird uses lichens to make a nest that is so small and camouflaged so well that you have to be very sharp to spot it. If you wear something red on our hike, you might find a hummingbird buzzing around you. Hummingbirds are attracted to red flowers for their nectar. These birds are extremely protective of their habitat in the forest. Each hummingbird stoutly defends its particular patch of flowers.

On our next stop in the temperate rain forest, you will need to lower your sights—but you won't need to lower your expectations. You will not be disappointed in what you see!

The secretive pine marten spends a great deal of time hunting squirrels and birds in the rainforest canopy.

Enchanted Garden

Is your neck getting stiff from looking up into the trees? Then let's look down for a change, at the third level of the Pacific Northwest rain forest, the understory and shrub layer. We can find an excellent example of this habitat in Queets Valley, between the Hoh Rain Forest and the Quinault Valley. First, however, we should take one last look up—at the biggest Douglas fir in Olympic National Park. It sits on the northern side of the Queets River Trail. This tree is 212 feet (65 m) tall and has a circumference of 534 inches (1,355 cm). That is 44 feet (13 m) around.

The vegetation of the temperate rain forest depends on sunlight. So it is not surprising that we will find a wealth of shrubs and other understory plants in the sunny openings along the banks of the Queets River and the many streams threading through the forest. Among the common shrubs here are Pacific rhododendron and azalea, known for their clusters of flowers, and salal, a species that has glossy leaves, bell-shaped blooms, and leathery dark blue berries. Huckleberries, salmonberries, blackberries, and thimbleberries are numerous, and their fruits feed birds and small mammals. The vine maple grows in

Ferns and mosses thrive along the banks of streams in Queets Valley.

gaps where light reaches the forest floor. This small airy tree is not really a vine, but sometimes a heavy load of epiphytes forces its slender branches to bend toward the forest floor, where they root and form vinelike arches.

Devil's club is another distinctive plant in this layer. It has huge, maplelike leaves and stems lined with long, sharp thorns. The oversized leaves allow the devil's club to thrive in the low light of the rain forest. Native Americans used the bark from the devil's club in medicines. Its red berries are a favorite food of bears and other mammals.

The Pacific yew grows in the understory of the temperate rain forest, rarely reaching more than 50 feet (15 m) in height. This tree produces a chemical called taxol in its bark and needles. Taxol can be used to help stop the spread of some types of cancer. Unfortunately, many Pacific yews were cut down to clear forest areas before we realized they were so valuable.

The large leaves of the devil's club help it gather light and collect moisture in the dim understory of the rain forest.

This patch of forest floor, choked with sword ferns, resembles a scene from the Carboniferous Period. Ferns so dominated that time period (360 to 286 million years ago) that it is often referred to as the "Age of Ferns."

With so much moisture and shade, it's not surprising to find lacy patches of ferns blanketing the rain forest. Sword ferns grow in abundance in the understory, sometimes reaching as high as 3 feet (1 m). Another species is appropriately called the deer fern because these plants attract black-tailed deer and elk.

Shaping the Landscape

Elk are master architects of the understory. Both elk and black-tailed deer browse on and trample the vegetation, keeping areas of the understory open. Without their browsing, the understory would quickly become overgrown and impenetrable for a variety of wildlife.

Elk are bigger than deer, so they have more of an impact on the forest. In fact, the elk in this region are the largest of all. They are called Roosevelt elk, after President Theodore Roosevelt. A bull, or male, Roosevelt elk can weigh as much as 1,000 pounds (450 kg), whereas a male black-tailed deer weighs from 120 to 250 pounds (57 to 120 kg). Elk herds live in Queets Valley year-round. A herd numbers from 15 to 30 animals, and they range over a territory of 6 to 12 square miles (15 to 31 sq km).

If you look around at the trees and shrubs, you can see the effect that elk have on the forest. They snip off the fronds of ferns and strip shrubs of their leaves. Some trees have no leaves or branches from ground level to about 6 feet (2 m) up. This is called the browse line and marks the highest level the elk can reach. Elk will even eat devil's club despite its sharp thorns.

The temperate rain forest is especially important to the elk as its winter habitat, after the grasses in the lush valleys have died. As winter progresses, the conifers of the temperate rain forest trap some of the falling snow up in the layers of the canopy. This means that the snow is not as deep in the forest as it is in the valley, so the elk can find lichens, mosses, and bark to eat more easily there.

During the 1980s, scientists decided to study the effects of elk browsing in the temperate rain forest. They surveyed two plots of land measuring 2.5 acres (1 ha) each, one in a grassy area along the river and one in a spruce-and-hemlock rain forest. The scientists identified

In the early 1900s, it was fashionable for men living in the cities of America to wear elk teeth. These canine teeth from the animal's upper jaw were worn dangling from gold watch chains. To meet the demand for these teeth, hunters killed the elk, took the teeth, and left the carcasses to rot. Stopping the slaughter was one of the reasons behind President Theodore Roosevelt's 1909 executive order creating Mount Olympus National Monument, the forerunner of Olympic National Park.

Elk help keep areas of the forest open, allowing plants and other animal species to thrive.

and counted all the different types of plants in each plot. Then they fenced off half of each plot so the elk could not feed in those areas. Soon, the scientists could see dramatic differences between the fenced and unfenced areas. In the enclosed sites, the plants grew taller and filled in open, grassy areas. The fenced-in deer ferns, for example, were twenty times taller than those growing outside the fences, where the elk could forage. But the diversity of plant species was much lower inside the fences. Browsing by the elk helps keep spaces open in the understory and encourages different varieties of plants to grow, which provides more habitats for other species of animals.

Making Music

One of the loveliest sounds in the temperate rain forest understory is the warble of the winter wren. This bird is only 4 inches (10 cm) long, but it has a loud, clear voice. It is a good thing because otherwise you might never know it has a habitat in this ecosystem. Dark reddish brown, the winter wren often sits inconspicuously on a branch in the shade of the understory. If you are lucky, however, it will emerge and sit on a fallen log. As it offers up its melody, the tiny bird holds its head back and shakes its tail vigorously.

The winter wren shares its habitat in the understory with the fox sparrow. This bird is also dark brown and has spots on its breast. Its song is a loud series of short notes and sliding whistles. Though it hides and sings in the understory, the fox sparrow looks for seeds in the needles and other litter on the forest floor. If you stand very still, you might see it kicking up the debris with both feet at the same time.

It is raining now, so we can hear the male Pacific tree frog giving his call, *krr-r-r-ek*. During the spring, the males begin singing loud choruses of their breeding call, particularly on rainy nights. Does it sound familiar? You may have heard it before because filmmakers often use these frog choirs as background sounds in movies. The 2-inch (5-cm) Pacific tree frog is the most common frog in the Pacific Northwest. It is bright green and has a dark line, like a mask, that runs from its nostrils to its shoulders. Sticky pads on the frog's toes help it climb about on branches, trunks, and shrubs, as it looks for spiders and insects. The Pacific tree frog depends on the rain forest to

Sticky pads on the toes of the Pacific tree frog help it climb among the understory.

keep its skin and eggs moist. It has found a perfect habitat in the damp understory with its many rushing streams.

What is left now to explore in the temperate rain forest? You are standing on it!

Carpet of Green

A small strip of temperate rain forest hugging the west coast of the Olympic Peninsula is also part of Olympic National Forest. To get there, we drive across a large area that once was covered by a lush forest. This area is outside the national park and has been logged for lumber. This bare area strikes a stark contrast with the cool, damp, quiet woods we have just left. It is a relief to return to the misty forest again as we begin looking along a mile-long trail to First Beach.

The serene forest floor is upholstered in soft vegetation that has magical sounding names such as haircap moss, wood nymphs, and maidenhair ferns. Foamflower and bunchberry are two of the many flowering plants that carpet the ground. Skunk cabbage grows in areas of standing water amid the cedar and spruce trees. As its name implies, the flower of this plant has a distinctive—and unpleasant—odor.

Fallen logs and large branches are scattered across the trail. They make walking a little difficult, but this woody debris is essential to life on the forest

Old-growth forests seem to have changed little in the hundreds of years it took them to develop. In truth, they are dynamic places, where nutrients from decaying matter are constantly being recycled into the soil.

floor. Dying and dead material is not wasted here. Through decomposition, the nutrients that the wood gathered while it was still alive are slowly released back into the soil. Coralroot, for example, often grows at the bases of the large trees. An orchid, it obtains its nutrients from the decaying organic matter on the forest floor.

Trees continue to contribute to the ecosystem for decades after they fall. Lying this way and that, the logs form natural terraces and stabilize the ground. Because the forest floor is always wet, the logs stay moist, providing habitats for animal species that require a damp environment. Invertebrates such as termites, carpenter ants, and bark beetles use these fallen logs as their primary source of food. They eat the wood, carving homes for other creatures. Witches butter, a bright yellow jelly fungus, thrives on dead wood. Lichens and mosses sprout there as well, slowly creeping up and over the logs.

Like the canopy-dwelling red tree vole, the red-backed vole prefers to dine on one specific food—in this case, truffles. Considered delicacies by people as well, truffles are fruiting bodies of a type of fungus that forms a relationship with the roots of conifers and other plants. Truffles fruit underground and cannot depend on wind to disperse their seed spores. Instead, they emit strong odors that attract red-backed voles and other mammals to dig them up and eat them. The truffle spores are spread by the voles into cleared areas, where they can germinate.

Under Our Feet

Now, you will have to use your imagination, because under our feet lies a nearly invisible ecosystem that helps support the entire forest. Small insects and **microorganisms**, such as tiny fungi and bacteria, are living directly below us. One type of fungus, **mycorrhizae**, forms a partnership with the roots of trees. Mycorrhiza means "fungus root," and it describes the **symbiosis**, or mutually beneficial relationship, that forms between the fungus and the roots. The threadlike fungi wrap around the tree roots and help the tree absorb water and nutrients, such as phosphorus and nitrogen, from the soil. Sometimes, the fungi link trees through an underground network. The trees, in turn, help feed the fungi with the sugars they make through photosynthesis. One Douglas fir tree may form partnerships with more than 2,000 different species of fungi.

Water is one of the keys to the temperate rain forest's success.

Fantastic Fungi

Fungi are a group of plants that includes mushrooms and molds. There are more than 50,000 different types of fungi. Unlike green plants, molds and other fungi cannot make their own food because they do not contain chlorophyll. Instead, fungi absorb nutrients from things such as rotting fruits and other organisms. Fungi play an important role in the Pacific Northwest rainforest ecosystem by decomposing the organic materials on the ground and returning nutrients to the soil. Fungi help in the process of breaking dead plant and animal matter into simpler components so the nutrients can be used by other organisms.

To find out what fungi look like and how they grow, you will need:

- a large clear plastic bag and a twist tie
- a cup of soil
- a piece of food, such as a slice of apple, cheese, or bread
- a magnifying glass
- a paper towel
- water

1. Place the soil in the plastic bag.

2. Place the piece of food on the soil.

3. Dampen the paper towel and place it in the bag.

4. Let some air into the plastic bag and secure the top with the twist tie. Do not blow into the bag, but just make sure there is some air inside.

5. Put the bag in a warm, dark place and let it sit for several days.

6. After a few days, check the bag. Do not open the bag or touch the contents. Look at the soil and the piece of food with your magnifying glass. You should see different types of fungi, or molds, growing on both the food and the soil.

Molds are made up of millions of spores, or tiny seeds, that grow together in a colony. Each of these spores can grow into a new mold. In the forest, molds form new colonies when the wind or an animal transports them to new sites.

Small creatures with a big job to do, millipedes process nutrients that will make it to the tops of the tallest trees.

The millipede is one of the most important of the many small creatures that live below the surface. The bright yellow-and-black cyanide millipede shreds the needles and leaves that fall from the trees, breaking them down into smaller bits that can be eaten by other organisms. In this way the millipede, beetles, and other tiny organisms recycle the nutrients that enable the trees to grow to enormous heights. Though this "world" is nearly invisible to us, it is extremely vital to the forest.

Wet and Wild

The damp environment of the forest floor is an ideal habitat for amphibians. Because their skin must stay moist, amphibians need water or the protective cover of moist logs and other debris to survive. Frog and salamander eggs hatch in the many streams running through the rain forest.

Let's turn over one of the small logs along the path and see what is underneath. There scurrying away is a western red-backed salamander, one of the most common and widespread species of woodland salamanders in the region. This 4-inch-long (10-cm) slender salamander has a reddish to yellowish stripe running from its head to the tip of its tail. It eats mites and other small invertebrates, including earthworms and spiders. Unlike many other species of salamanders, the western red-backed salamander does not lay its eggs in water. Rather, the female lays her clutch in a moist place on the forest floor. We must be sure to replace the log so we do not disturb the natural habitat of the salamander and the many other creatures living under the log.

One of the most distinctive salamanders in this habitat is the rough-skinned newt. It is the only salamander in this temperate rain forest that is active during the day. This newt also differs from others in that it has dry, rough skin. It is large for an amphibian, nearly 8 inches (20 cm) long. In the spring, rough-skinned newts gather at ponds in the forest to breed and lay their eggs. If you surprise the newt, it may raise its head and tail, flatten its body against the ground, and close its eyes. This defense posture exposes the newt's bright orange undersides, which may scare off a predator. This is a warning to you, too. Do not pick it up! Rough-skinned newts have skin glands that produce a dangerous poison. Legend has it that some Pacific Northwest Indians used the toxin from newts to poison the tips of their arrows.

There is a small stream up ahead. We will find different amphibian species there. If the water is cold enough, we may locate an Olympic torrent salamander. Its habitat is in or near cold, clear streams and waterfalls. The adults almost always live in the splash zone, where a thin trickle of water runs between the rocks. The young, on the other hand, are found in deeper water. During really wet weather, these salamanders may leave the streams and go out into the forest. Torrent salamanders cannot survive where temperatures are too high. When trees are cut down along the banks of streams, increased sunlight may make the water too warm for this species.

If we turn over a rock in the stream, we may find a tailed frog.

The presence of Olympic torrent salamanders is a good indication the ecosystem is healthy. There are enough trees shading the stream, so the water temperature is stable and suitable for the species.

The male of this species is easy to identify, as it is the only adult frog with a short, stumpy tail. It is not a true tail, but a fleshy appendage used in breeding. Tailed frog tadpoles have adapted to living in swift-flowing forest streams by developing suckerlike mouths that enable them to cling to rocks. The lungs of the adult frog are small, but the frog can absorb the oxygen in the water through its skin rather than having to come up for air. The frog's "fingertips" are hard, like claws, and help it crawl among the rocks on the stream bottom. Unlike most other frogs, the tailed frog is voiceless—another adaptation to its habitat of noisy, rushing streams in the temperate rain forest. In short, the frog eventually lost its voice as it wouldn't be of much use in such a loud environment.

Fish Tales

Forest debris plays a large role in creating habitats in the many streams running through this ecosystem. Where leaves and other organic matter accumulate in a stream, they create steps, gravel bars, and pools that are important in the life cycle of salmon and other fish.

Salmon, in particular, use the calm waters in these pools as egg-laying sites.

Logging that results in bare stream banks affects fish as well as salamanders. If erosion and runoff allow too much soil to enter the water, the fish may suffocate. Likewise, without the gradual steps formed by debris and deposits of sediment, the fish may not be able to complete their swim upstream in the fast-running water.

A hundred years ago, the Pacific rain forest and its many rivers supported huge numbers of salmon. After spending their adult lives at sea, salmon swim back up these rivers to the places where they were born to lay their eggs and die. Dams built over the past one hundred years have blocked many of these rivers. Loggers have also clear-cut the trees lining the banks of the rivers, causing soil to wash into the water. In 1999, nine of the rivers used by salmon were included in the U.S. Endangered Species Act in order to protect them.

In order to spawn, or lay their eggs, red salmon must migrate from the salt water of the ocean to a freshwater stream. Their bodies are able to adapt to these drastically different environments.

49

   As we approach the coast and look at the beach, we see that logs, branches, and entire trees have washed down the river systems or toppled over the edge of the cliff above the beach. This dead wood is used by birds such as blue herons and eagles as resting sites and hunting perches. When the logs are washed out to sea, entire communities develop around these nutrient-rich life rafts. Tuna and other large fish may rest under the floating logs. Even after the rainforest trees sink to the bottom of the ocean, their nutrients continue to recycle, contributing to the health of other ecosystems.

Debris litters the beaches bordering the temperate rain forests. Just like fallen logs in the forest, these dead trees have not outlived their usefulness to the coastal communities. A variety of organisms will burrow beneath or perch on top of them.

Tomorrow's Temperate Rain Forests

*W*here do the Douglas fir and western red cedar boards used in building our houses, decks, and furniture come from? They come from the temperate rain forests such as the one we have been visiting in Olympic National Park. This forest ecosystem once stretched unbroken for 2,000 miles (3,200 km) along the west coast of North America, from northern Oregon to Alaska. The rain forest protected in Olympic National Park is a small part of the whole ecosystem. Much of the rest of the ecosystem is at risk of being destroyed. About 30 million acres (12 million hectares) of old-growth forest existed in 1890. More than 80 percent of that has been harvested already. Virtually all of the temperate rain forest remaining in the region is now on federal lands, most of it in national forests but not in national parks. There are important distinctions between a national forest and a national park. The United States has 156 national forests. Unlike national parks in which commercial use of natural resources is prohibited, national forests are managed for what is called **multiple use**.

A path invites the curious to explore the wonders of a temperate rain forest.

That means that this land and its resources, like those in national parks, can be used by people for recreation, hiking, hunting, fishing, and wildlife watching. However, it also means they can be used for logging, grazing by livestock, and mining. More than 20 percent of the country's commercial forest land lies within the national forests. The nation's largest national forest is the Tongass in Alaska. This reserve was created in 1902. Officially named the Tongass National Forest in 1907, it covers 17 million acres (6.8 million ha) of the northernmost temperate rain forest in the world. It extends 500 miles (800 km) north of where we have been exploring along the Olympic Peninsula.

Cutting Edges

Since the pioneers first reached the seemingly endless expanse of tall trees and lush rain forest in the Pacific Northwest, the cutting of these trees has been relentless. Not only the temperate rain forest, but all the world's forests are disappearing as the human population grows and the demand for wood increases. As the oldest, straightest, and most valuable of the rainforest trees are cut down, the commercial value of the remaining old-growth trees skyrockets.

Modern forestry practices—especially clear-cutting (removing all the trees, not just the commercially valuable ones)—destroy and fragment wildlife habitats, thus reducing the biodiversity in an ecosystem. Not all the wood in a clear-cut is used. Wood that is not hauled away is wasted or burned, sending great amounts of carbon into the atmosphere. Releasing all that carbon may speed up the destruction of the ozone layer that protects Earth's atmosphere, thus hastening global warming. That means that the air temperature will become warmer everywhere, including the cool temperate rain forest. Sitka spruce, Douglas fir, club mosses, and other plants that grow only in this climate will disappear, leaving northern spotted owls, marbled murrelets, and chickaree with no place to live.

Loggers have left some trees standing, but there are not always enough to prevent soil erosion and the other effects of clear-cutting.

Where the trees have been clear-cut on steep slopes, the thin soil washes away into streams and chokes the salmon, tailed frogs, and other species that live there. Or the soil fills in areas and destroys valuable nesting and feeding sites. The wooded areas that border the clear-cuts become drier and windier than the temperate rain forest. Deer and some species of birds that live primarily on the perimeters of the forests will thrive in these areas. But the forests themselves become less hospitable for the Vaux's swifts and torrent salamanders that depend on the old growth of the Pacific Northwest temperate rain forest.

Recycling Center

Beyond providing habitats for plant and animal species, the rain forest of the Pacific Northwest makes life on Earth better for humans as well. The forest is a champion at recycling. Through photosynthesis, the trees absorb the excess carbon in the atmosphere and pump life-sustaining oxygen into the air. The leaves and needles also collect dust and other particles from the air. The forest filters water from rainstorms and slowly releases it into the ground, reducing soil erosion and mud slides. It continually returns nutrients to the environment.

In 1990, conservationists fought to change the logging and timber sale practices in the Tongass. A compromise was reached, and the Tongass Timber Reform Act was passed. It called for protection of some of the rain forest by establishing wilderness areas. To date, 5.7 million acres (2.31 million ha) have been set aside in 19 wilderness areas. Among them is Alaska Chilkat Bald Eagle Preserve, where more than 3,000 eagles flock to a 5-mile (8-km) stretch of river to feed on salmon from October to January. Large numbers of grizzly bears wander through another area, Admiralty Island National Monument. Wolves and mountain goats live in the forest habitats of Misty Fiords National Monument. Outside the nineteen protected areas, however, the rest of the Tongass National Forest remains open to use by loggers, miners, and other commercial interests. If logging is allowed to continue at the current rate throughout the national forest system, old-growth forests will survive only in pockets of national parks and in small protected areas.

A unique ecosystem thousands of years in the making, once a forest is cut down, it is impossible to re-create the countless habitats it contains.

Shrinking Habitats

As humans cut down more and more of the temperate rain forest in the Pacific Northwest, the plants and animals there have less and less room. National parks and reserves, such as Olympic National Park, protect wildlife habitats, but these areas may become isolated islands surrounded by development. As the forest disappears, what happens to the wildlife living in this ecosystem? This activity will help you and five or more of your friends find out.

You will need:

- a name tag for each participant
- colored cards, one color each to represent food, water, and shelter (You will need enough of each color to play several rounds. If there are six players, you need six of each color for round one.)
- twine or rope measuring about 15 yards (14 m)
- a large open area or a large room
- a box for collecting the cards between rounds

1. Players will each choose an animal of the temperate rain forest that they would like to be, such as a northern spotted owl or a red-backed vole. Write the animal's name on your name tag. You are that animal. To survive, you must find food, shelter, and water cards—one of each per round.

2. Have everyone stand in the center of the area. Scatter the cards and have all players look for one of each color. Then collect all the cards and take away one of each category. The habitat is shrinking.

3. Use the rope to make the playing area smaller. Scatter the remaining cards and see which "animals" can find a set of all three cards—food, shelter, and water. See who "survived" this round. Any animals with two or fewer cards must drop out. The habitat can no longer support them.

4. Again take away a card from each color, making the playing area smaller, and play round three.

5. Make the area too small for the survivors to fit in. What happens when you run out of room? Can the northern spotted owl move to a different habitat?

The Forest Primeval

It has taken hundreds of years for the Sitka spruce, Douglas fir, and other trees in the Pacific Northwest temperate rain forest to grow large enough to maintain this ecosystem's delicate balance. It takes only minutes for loggers with chain saws to destroy the fragile life cycle. The end result of a deck on someone's house is a hole in the forest. We can plant more trees, but we cannot re-create the fragile, complex temperate rainforest ecosystem. The more we know about this ecosystem, the better prepared we will be to help preserve it.

Glossary

adaptation the special features developed by organisms to help them survive in a particular environment. For example, conifer trees are evergreen, which means they do not lose their leaves every year and therefore can produce food year-round.

amphibian an animal, such as a frog or a salamander, without scales that is adapted for life both in water and on land.

biodiversity the variety of plant and animal species in an area.

biomass living matter.

camouflage blending in with the surroundings through color or behavior modification.

canopy layer formed by the leaves and branches of the forest's trees, usually the emergent layer, or the layer formed by the tallest trees. The temperate rain forest also has midlevel and lower-level canopies.

clear-cut to remove all standing vegetation. This is generally the most profitable and frequently applied forestry technique in the Pacific Northwest.

conifer a cone-bearing tree, which usually has needle leaves and is evergreen. Examples are pines, firs, and spruces.

deciduous seasonal shedding of leaves, as oak trees lose their leaves every autumn.

decompose to decay or break down dead plant and animal material into simpler components so the materials can be used again. A dead log slowly decomposes or decays, returning its nutrients to the soil.

ecosystem the association of living things in a biological community, plus its interactions with the nonliving parts of the environment.

emergent layer the branches and leaves of the forest's tallest trees.

environment all the living and nonliving things that surround an organism and affect its life.

epiphyte a plant living on another plant.

erode to remove soil and rock by wind or water. Erosion is a natural process, but it can be very damaging if it occurs too rapidly.

evergreen having foliage that remains green and continues to produce food through photosynthesis year-round.

fern a plant that has leaflike fronds and reproduces by spores.

fungus a group of plants that includes mushrooms and molds, which help to decompose organic material, returning nutrients to the soil. The plural form is fungi.

habitat the place that has all the living and nonliving things that an organism needs to live and grow.

lichen a plant that is a combination of a fungus and an alga. Lichen commonly grows on trees and rocks.

microorganism an organism of microscopic or very tiny size.

moss a plant that grows in moist areas on soil, tree trunks, and rocks. Mosses lack true roots and depend on direct contact with surface moisture for water and nutrients.

multiple use when referring to national parks and protected areas, it means they can be used by commercial interests, such as logging and mining, as well as for recreation.

mycorrhizae an association between a type of fungus and tree roots underground.

nurse log a tree that has died, fallen, and begun to decompose, providing a moist elevated pile of fertilizer on which other plants can grow.

nutrient any organic molecule needed by a plant or animal.

photosynthesis the process by which plants and some other organisms that have chlorophyll use sunlight, carbon dioxide, and water to make sugars and other substances.

predator an animal that hunts or kills other animals for food. The northern spotted owl is a predator of mice and other small mammals.

snag a dead tree that is still standing, a hallmark of temperate rain forests.

species a group of organisms that closely resemble one another and can breed with each other to produce fertile offspring.

symbiosis a relationship between plants and/or animals.

temperate having a moderate, or relatively mild, climate.

understory the layer of the forest below the canopy where plants such as small trees, bushes, and grasses grow.

Further Exploration

Books

Alden, Peter, and Dennis Paulson. *National Audubon Society Field Guide to the Pacific Northwest*. New York: Alfred A. Knopf, 1998.

Ellis, Gerry, and Karen Kane. *America's Rainforest*. Minocqua, WI: North Word Press, Inc, 1991.

Kelly, David, and Gary Braasch. *Secrets of the Old Growth Forest*. Salt Lake City, UT: Peregrine Smith Press, 1988.

Kirk, Ruth, with Jerry Franklin. *The Olympic Rain Forest: An Ecological Web*. Seattle, WA: University of Washington Press, 1992.

McNulty, Tim. *Olympic National Park: A Natural History Guide*. Boston: Houghton Mifflin Company, 1996.

Organizations

Defenders of Wildlife
1101 14th Street N.W.
#1400
Washington, D.C. 20005
(202) 682-9400
www.defenders.org

Northwest Environment Watch
1402 Third Avenue, Suite 1127
Seattle, WA 98101-9743
(206) 447-1880
email: new@northwestwatch.org

Sierra Club
85 Second Street
Second Floor
San Francisco, CA 94105-3441
(415) 977-5500
www.sierraclub.org

Wilderness Society
900 Seventeenth Street N.W.
Washington, D.C. 20006
(800) THE-WILD
www.wilderness.org

Olympic National Park
600 East Park Avenue
Port Angeles, WA 98362-6798
(360) 452-4501
www.nps.gov/olym

Index

Page numbers for illustrations are in **boldface**.